ANATOMY AND PHYSIOLOGY FOR KIDS!

The Human Body and it Works

Children's Anatomy & Physiology Books

Speedy Publishing LLC

40 E. Main St. #1156

Newark, DE 19711

www.speedypublishing.com

Copyright 2016

We walk because we have feet.
We talk because we have a mouth.

Learn more about Body parts
and their function.

Body Parts

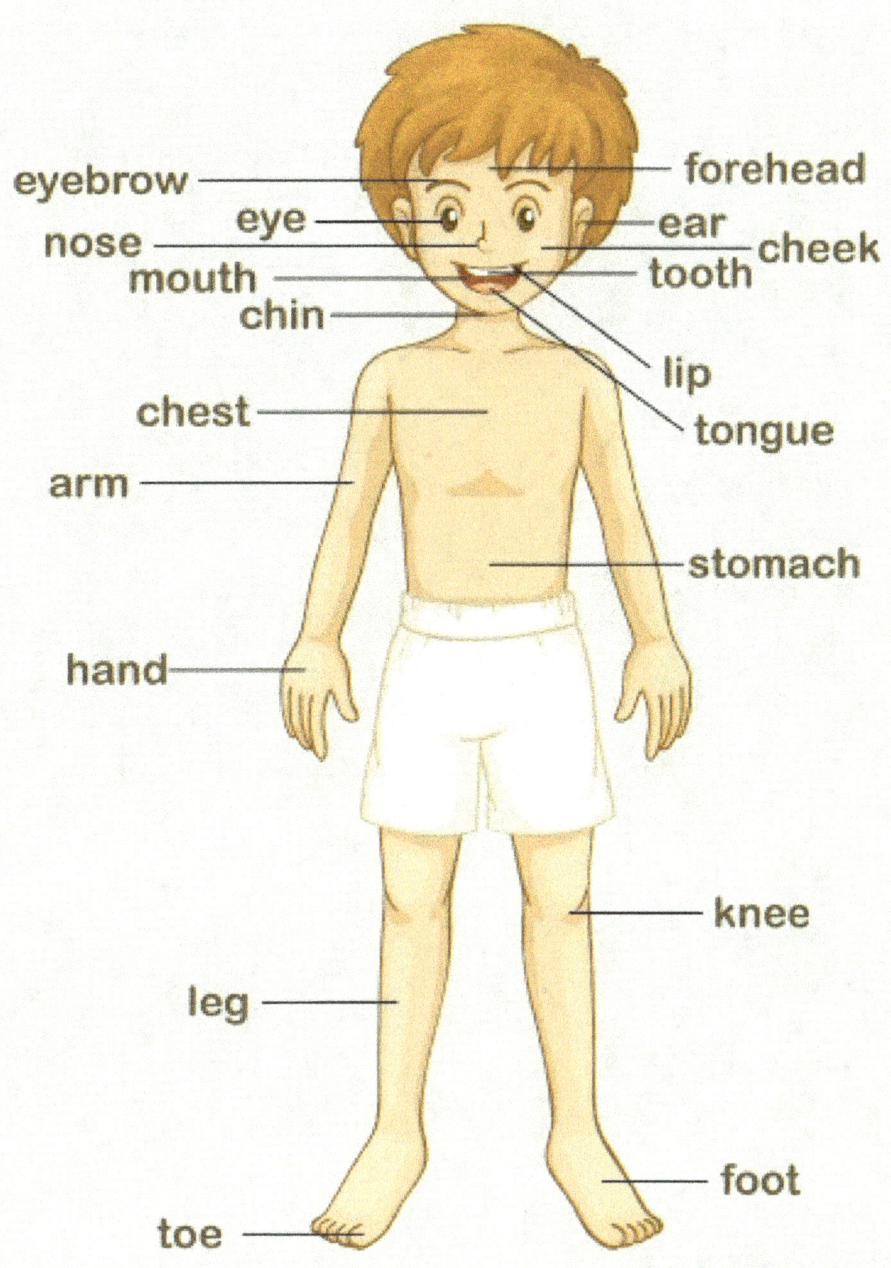

eyebrow
forehead
eye
nose
ear
cheek
mouth
tooth
chin
lip
tongue
chest
arm
stomach
hand
knee
leg
foot
toe

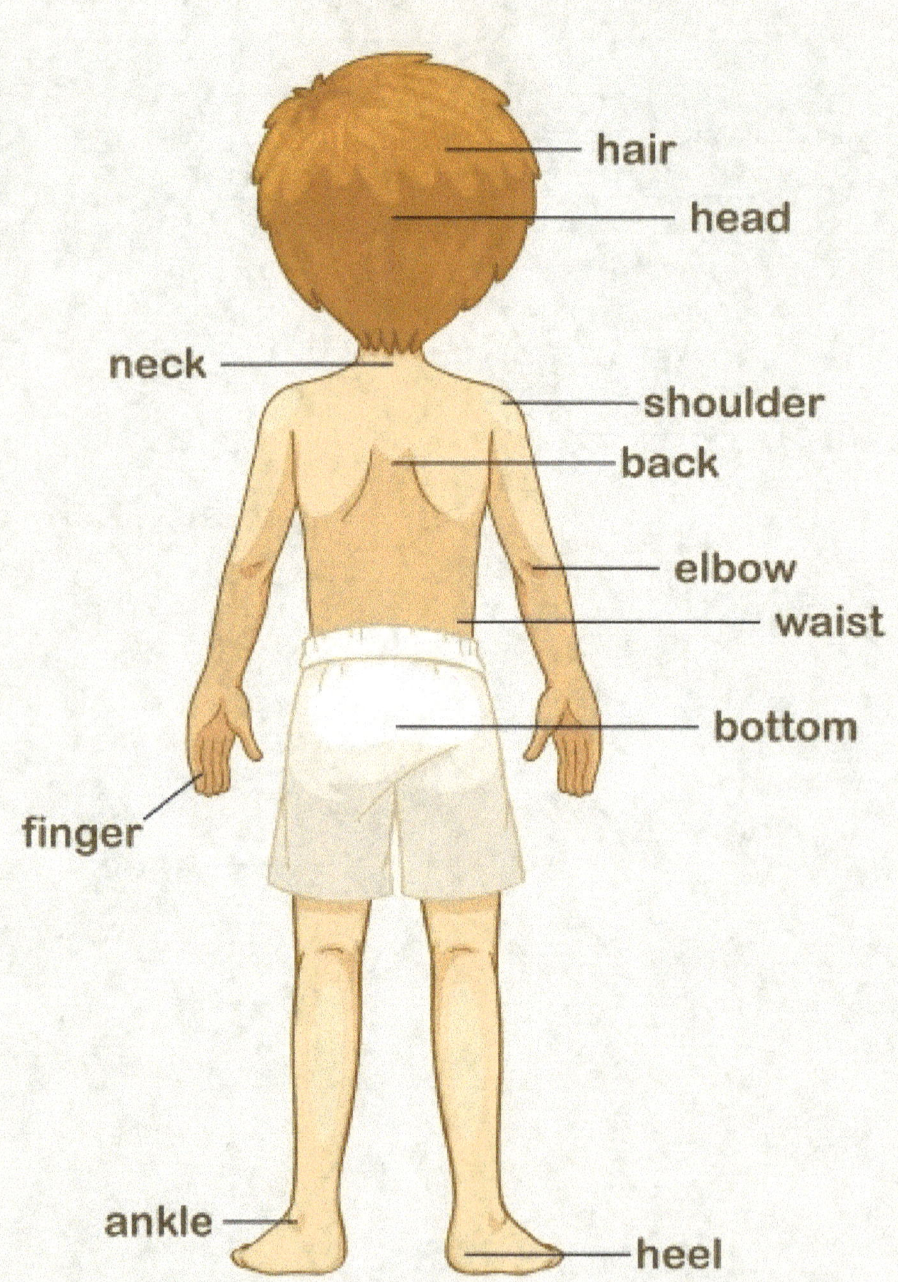

hair
head
neck
shoulder
back
elbow
waist
bottom
finger
ankle
heel

Functions and descriptions of the Body Parts.

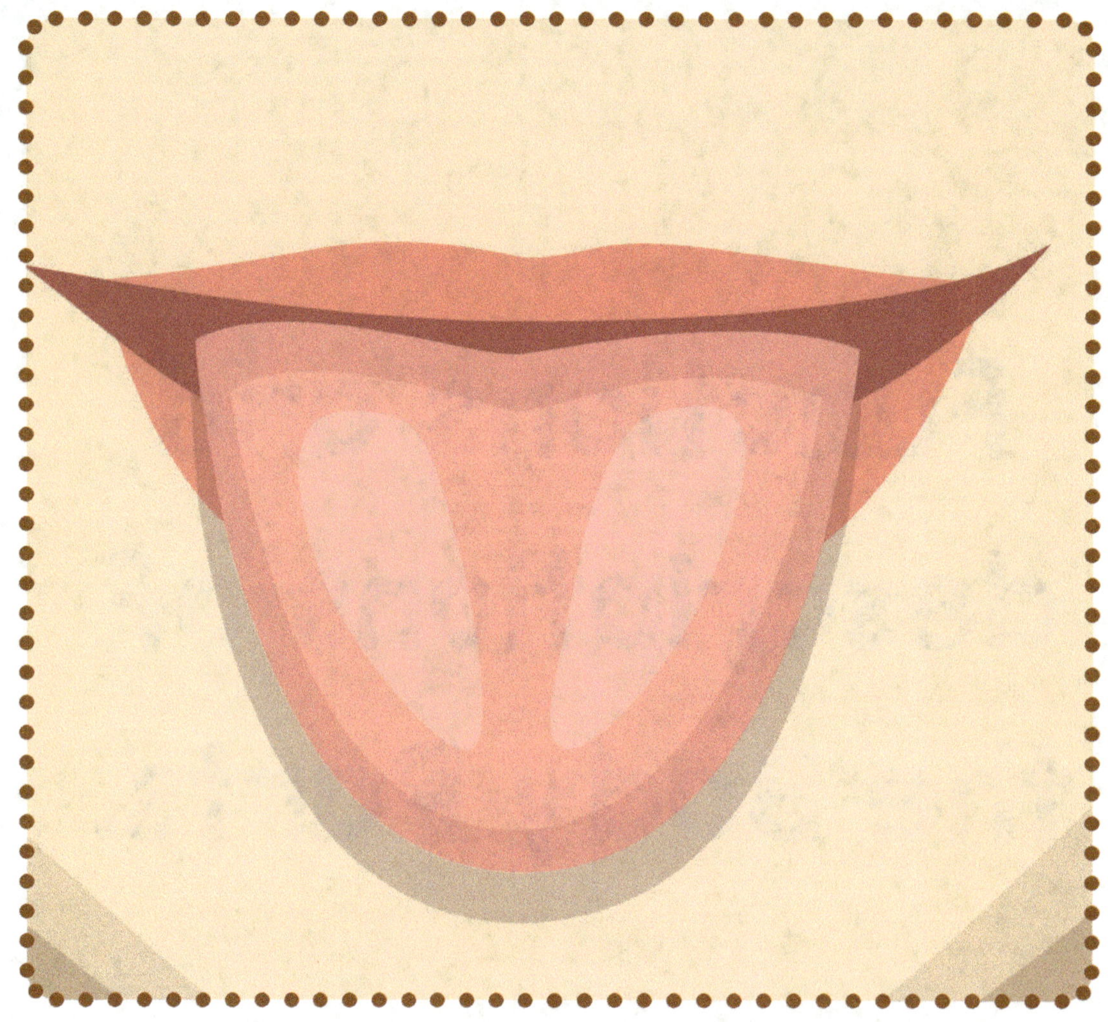

tongue

The tongue is used
to taste food.

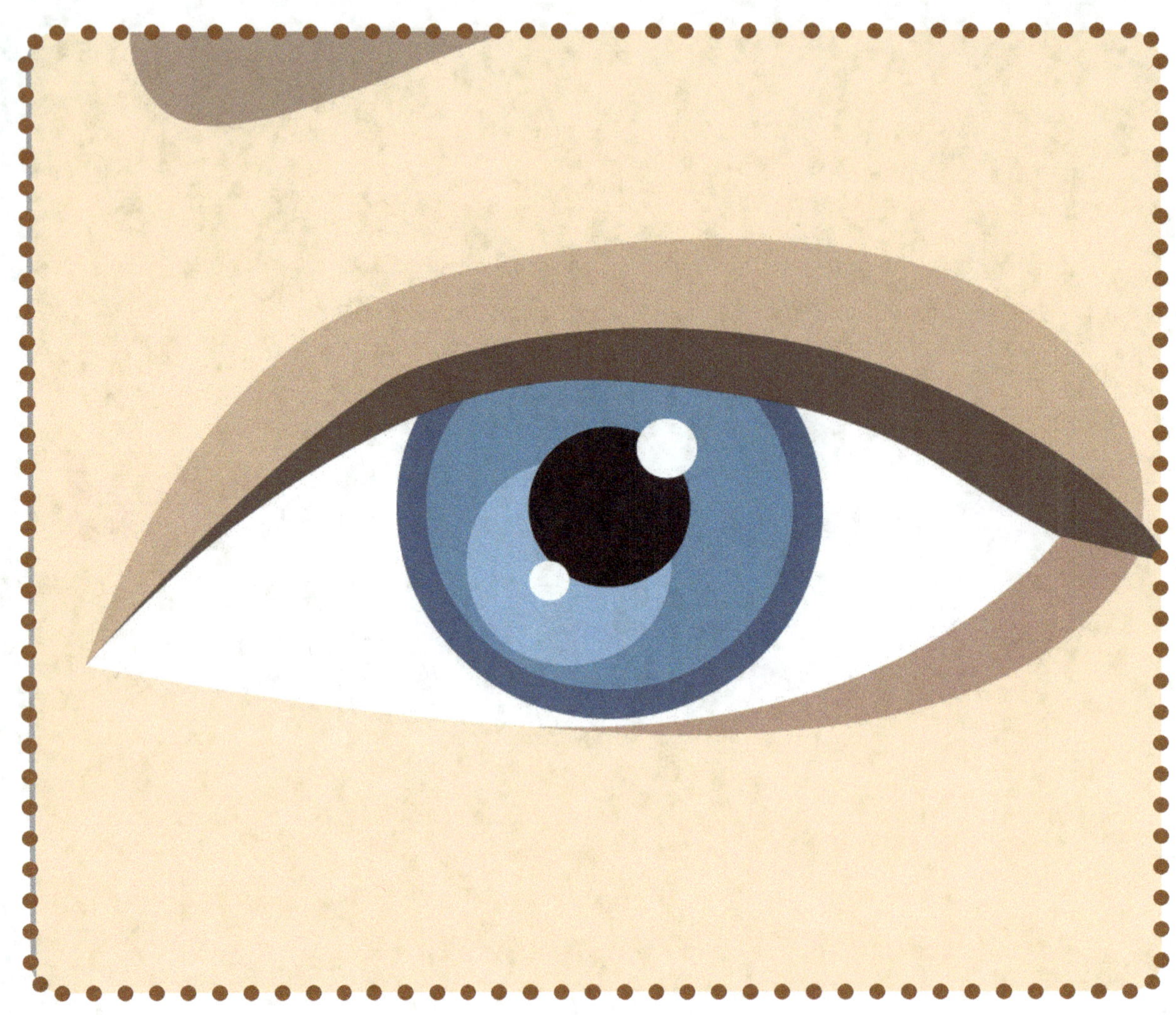

eye

The eyes detect
light and allow us
to see.

nose

The nose has short hairs inside to filter the dangerous particles inhaled.

Forehead

The muscles of the forehead help emphasize facial expression.

Neck

The neck supports
the head to maintain
its balance.

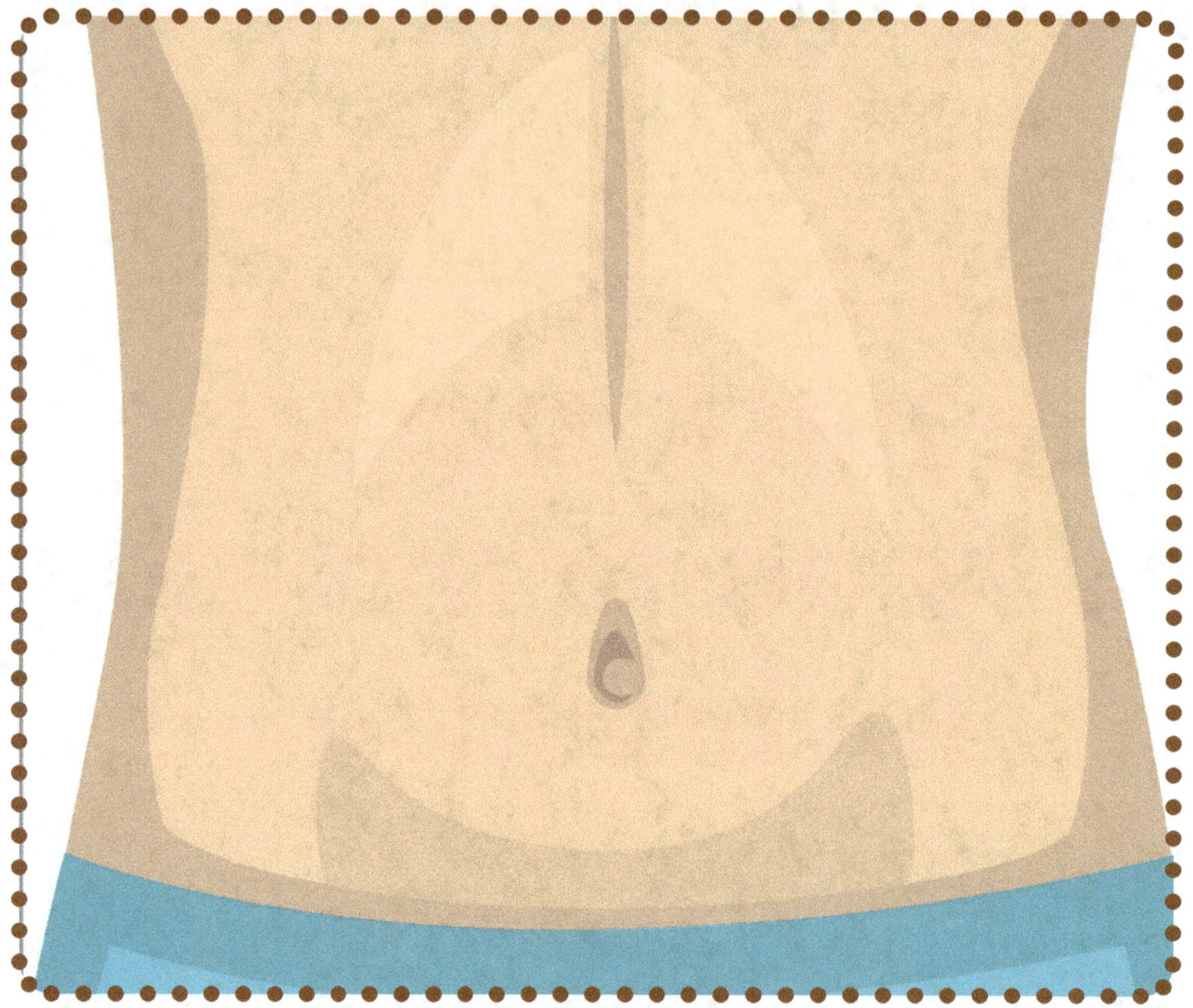

stomach

The stomach secretes acids to break food down for easier digestion.

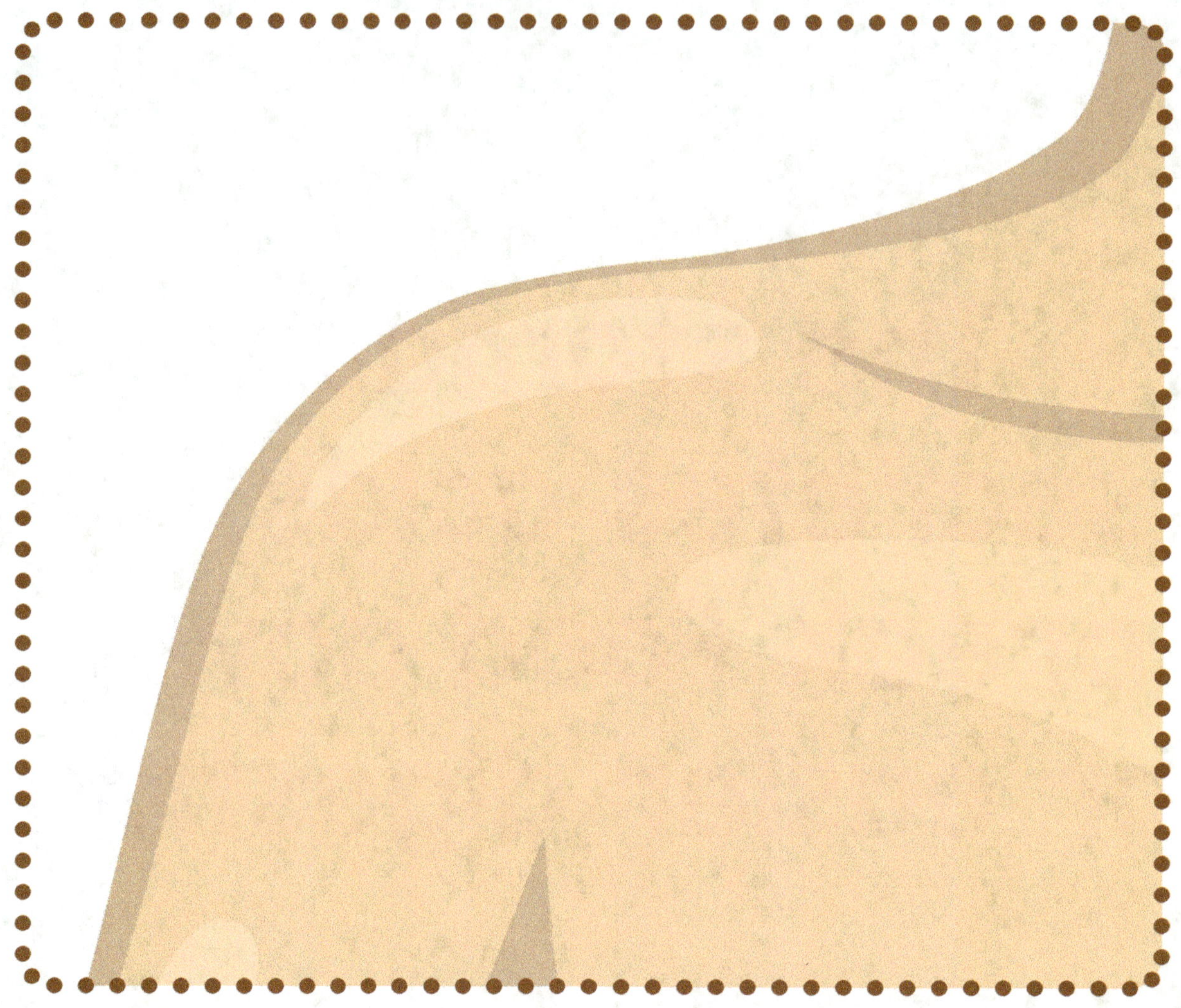

shoulder

The shoulder is
made up of clavicle,
collar bone and
scapulla.

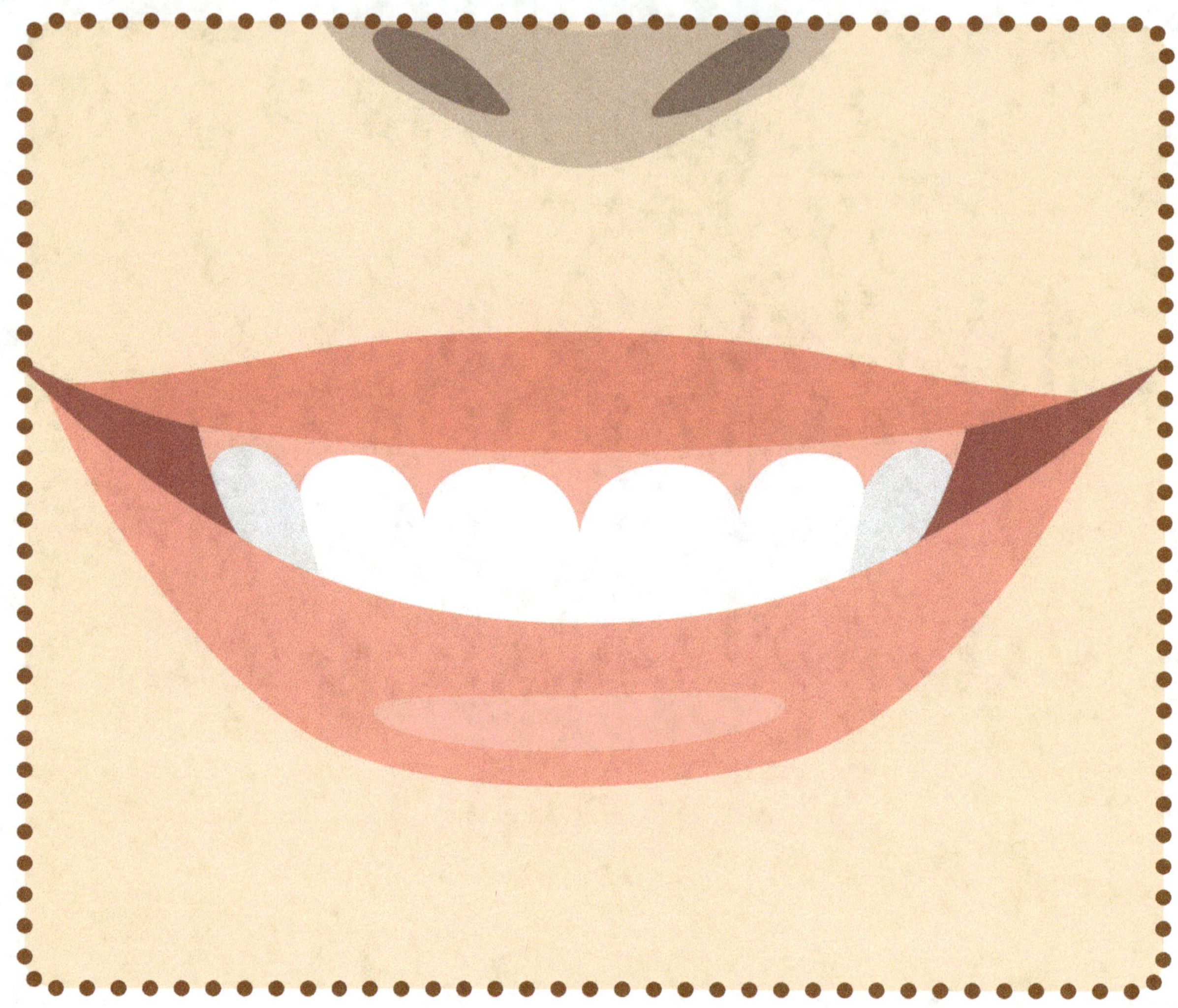

teeth

Teeth are harder and stronger than bones.

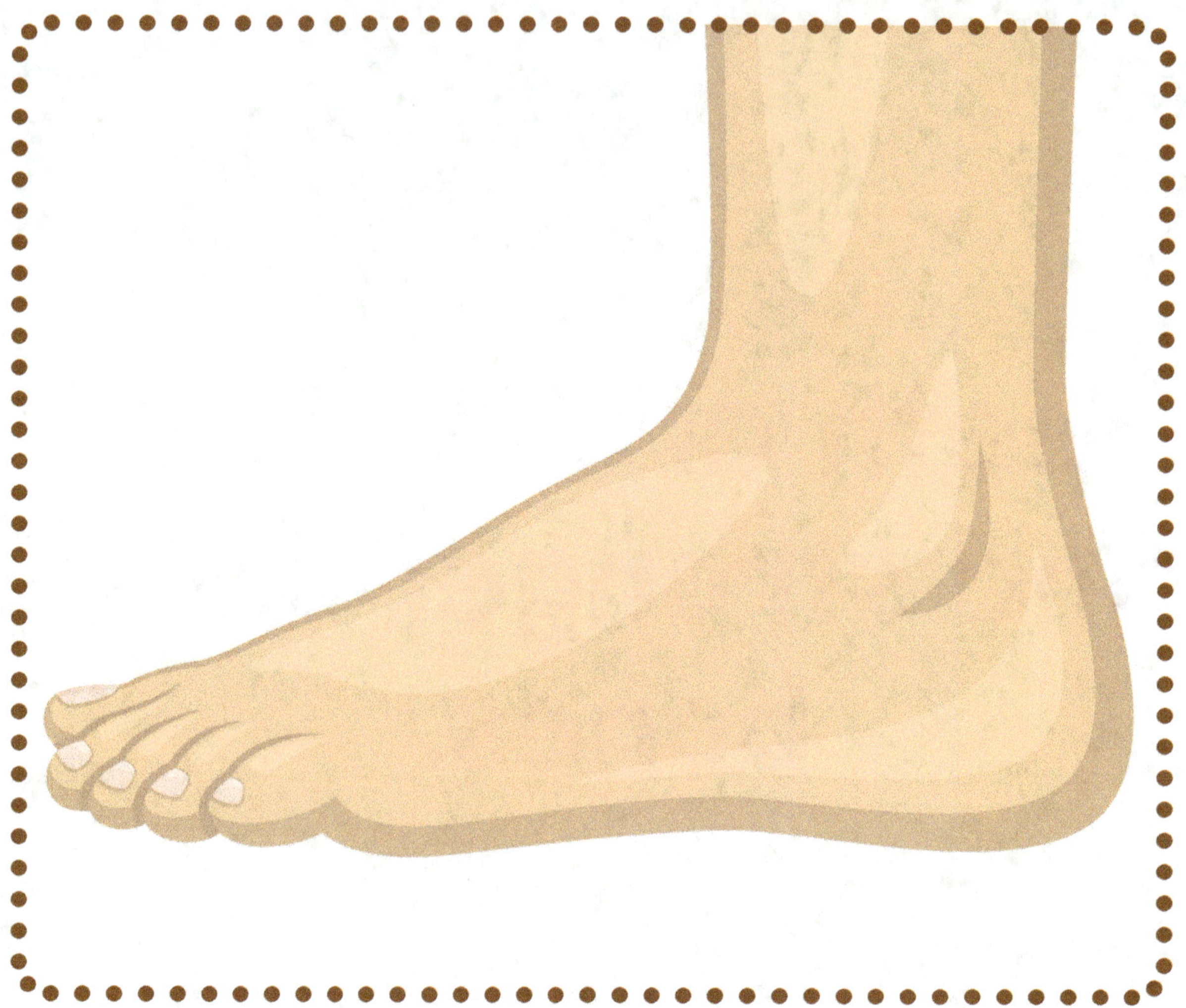

foot

A foot is one of the most ticklish part of the human body.

Finger

The finger contains
unique patterns and
these are called
Finger Prints.

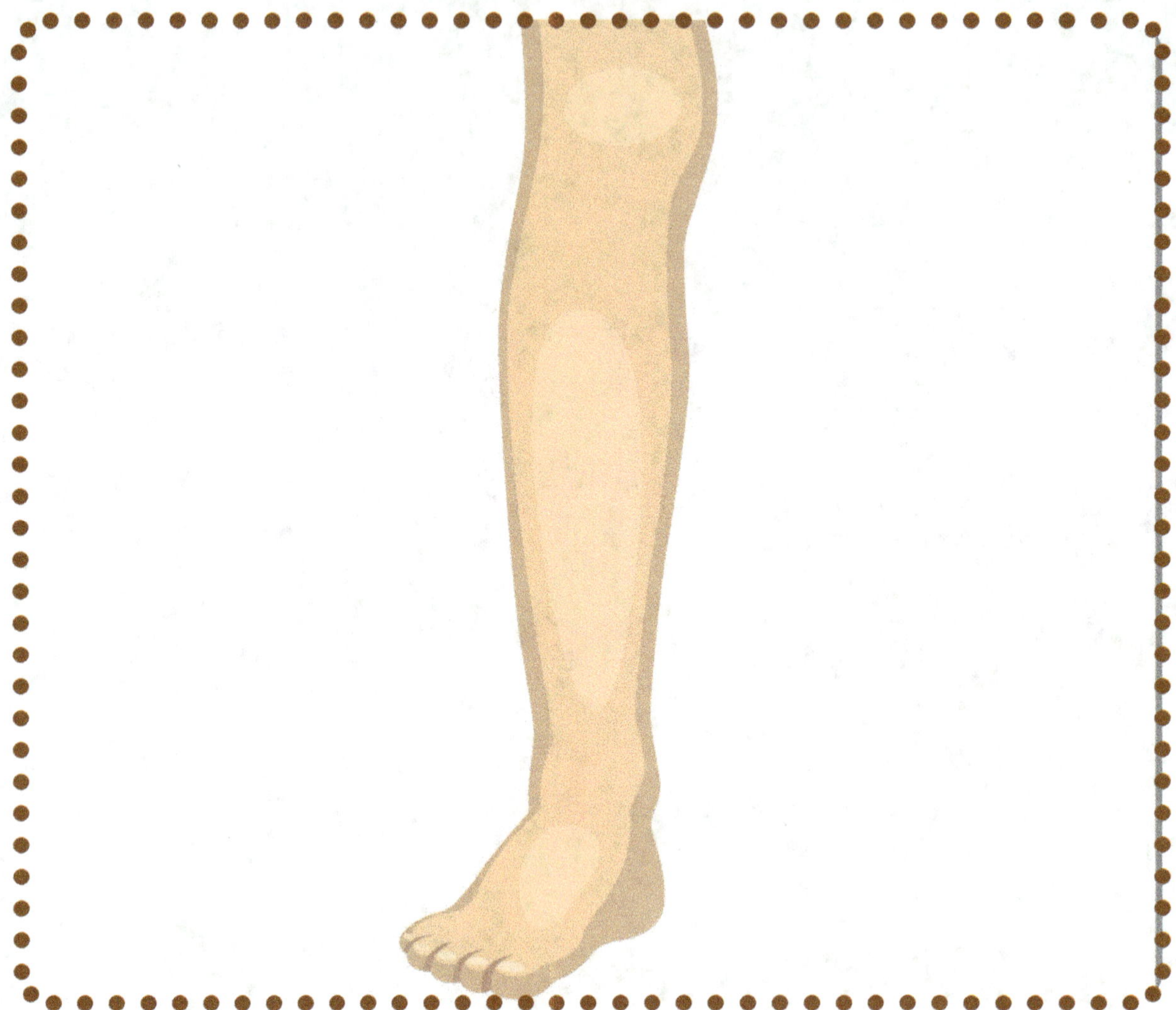

leg

The leg is used to walk, stand and run. Femur is the longest bone of the legs.

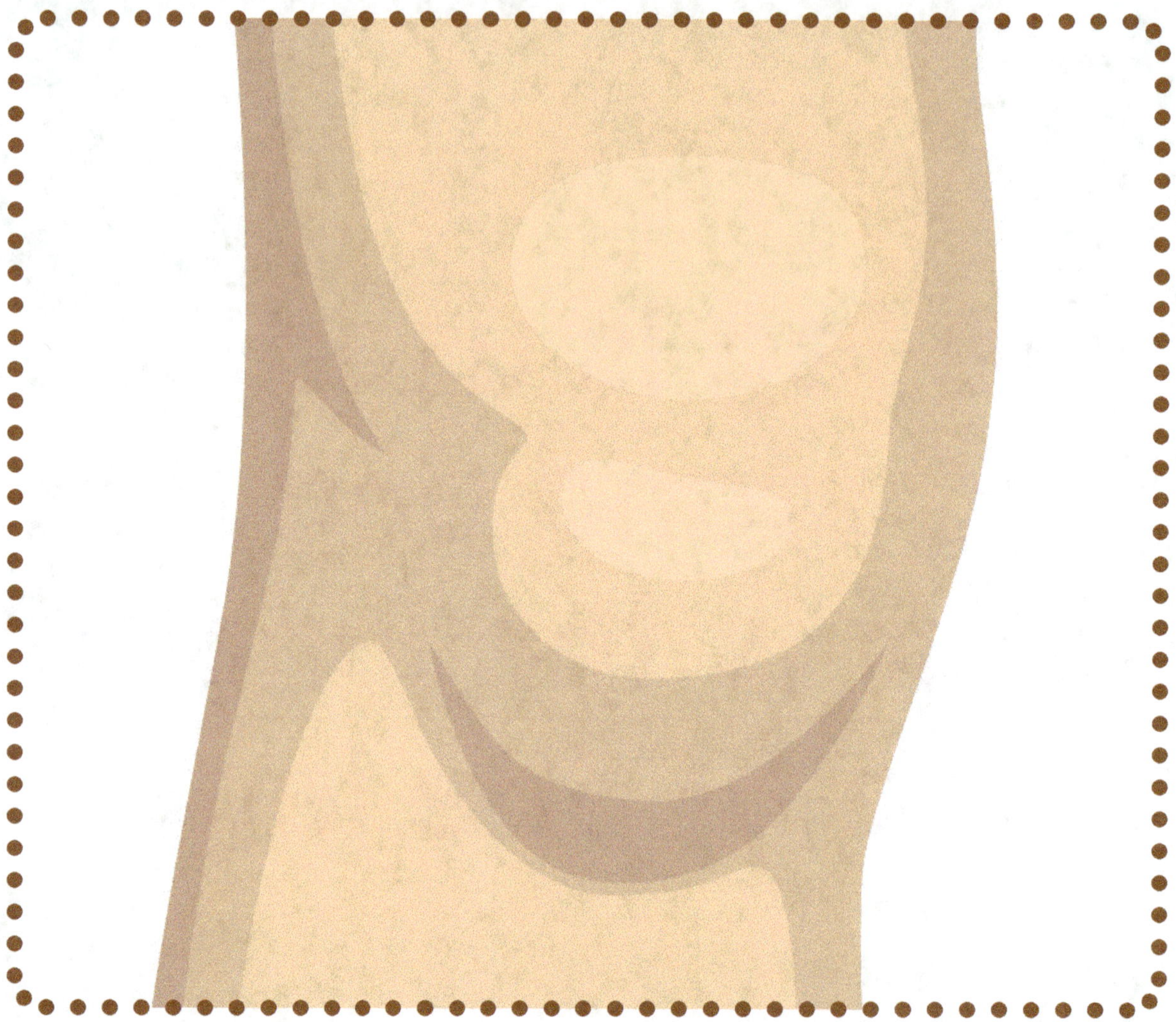

knee

The is knee composed of cartilage, ligaments, tendons and veins.

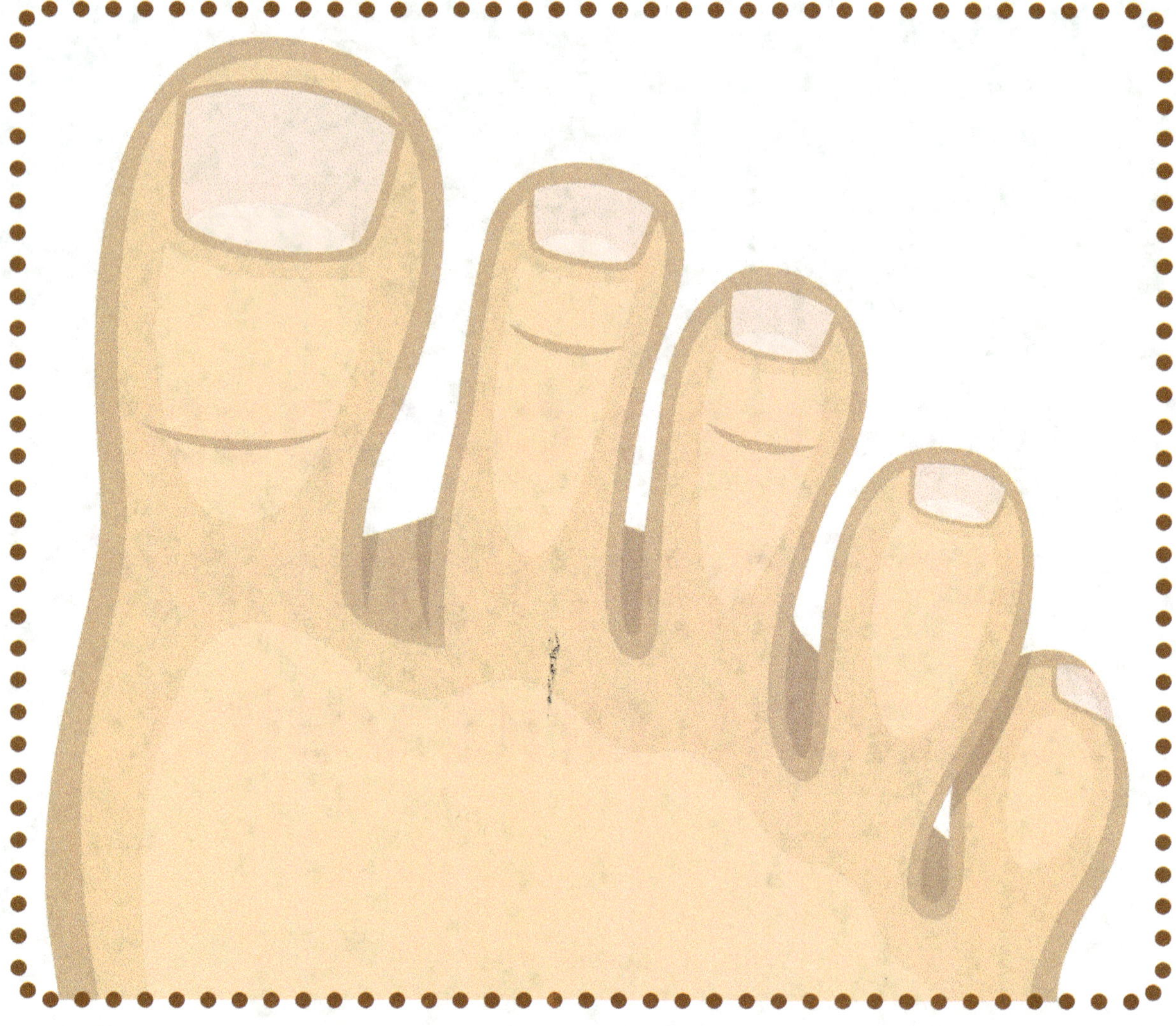

toes

The toes are like the fingers of your foot. Polydactyly is a condition when there is more than 5 toes in a foot.

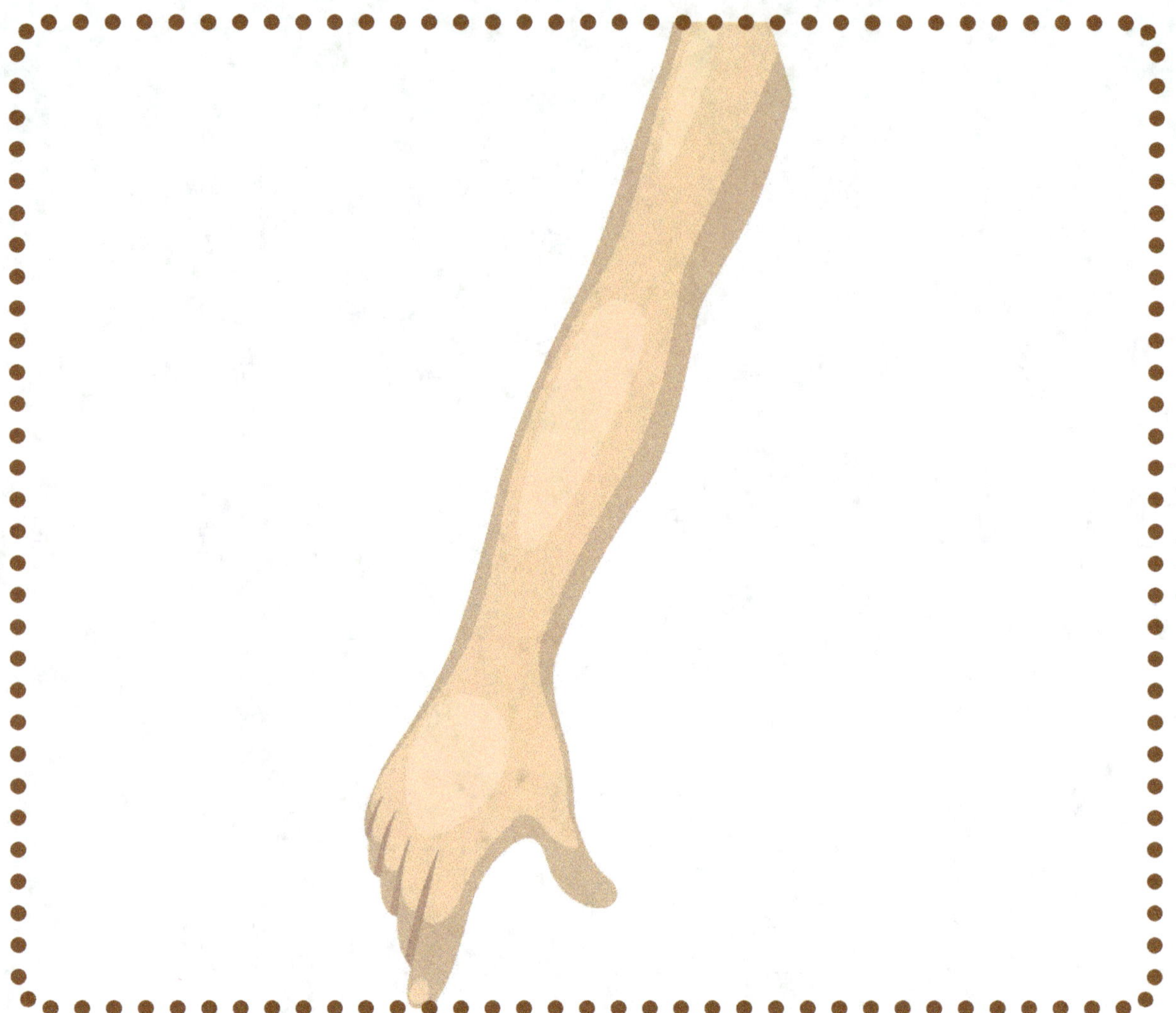

arm

The arm is the upper limb of the body.

chest

The chest is the part between your neck and stomach that contains your heart.

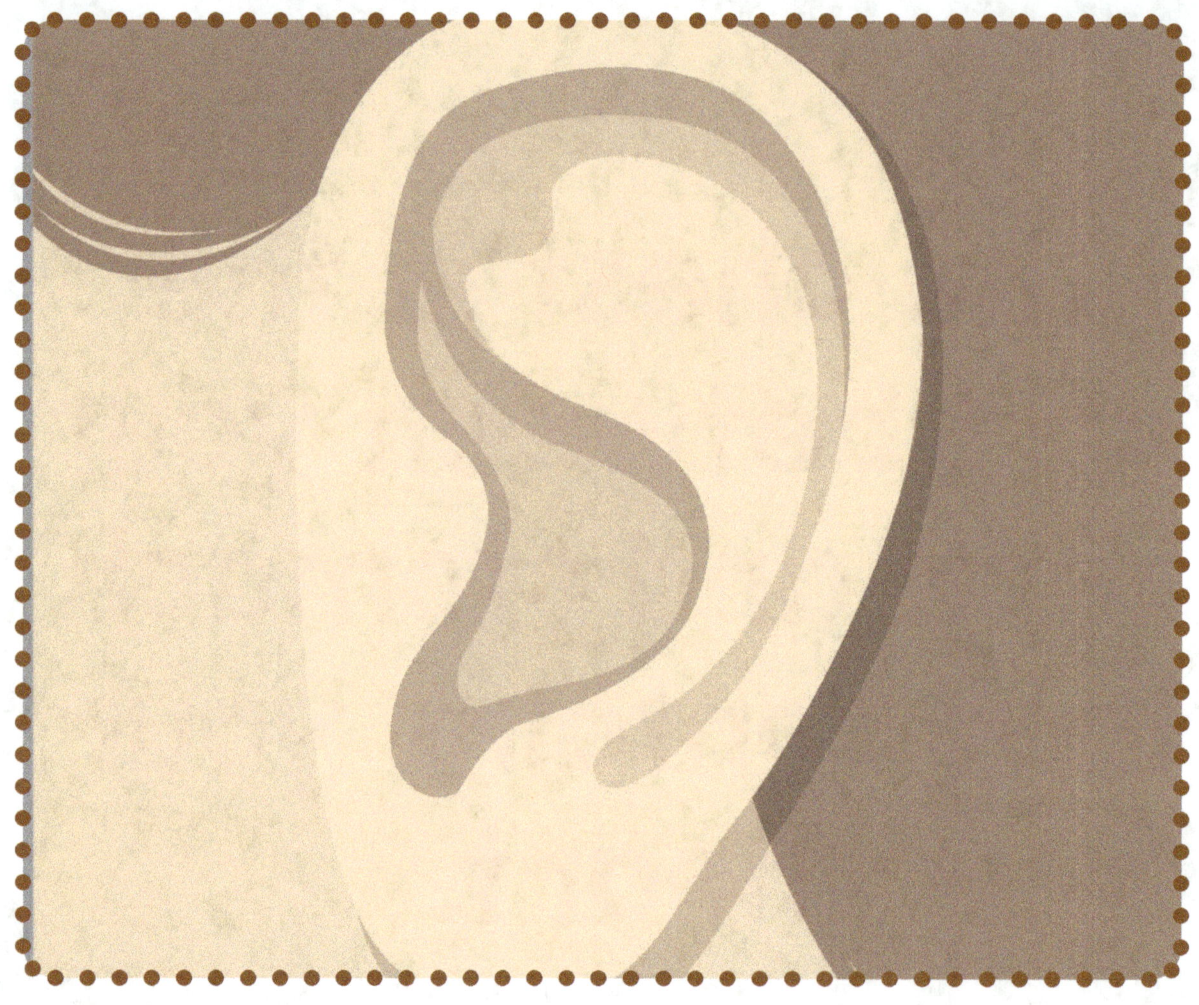

ear

The ear provides us
with our sense of
balance.

Tell your friends
about what you
learned from this
book.

Happy Sharing!

Visit

BABY PROFESSOR
EDUCATION KIDS

www.BabyProfessorBooks.com
to download Free Baby Professor eBooks
and view our catalog of new and exciting
Children's Books